MYSTERIES OF PLANET EARTH

ALSO BY FRANKLYN M. BRANLEY

MYSTERIES OF PLANET EARTH

Franklyn M. Branley

Diagrams by Sally J. Bensusen

LODESTAR BOOKS   E. P. DUTTON   NEW YORK

Fields Corner

*Jacket photo: A view of Earth as photographed
from the Apollo 17 spacecraft.* NASA

*Photograph on opposite page
courtesy of Hale Observatories*

Text copyright © 1989 by Franklyn M. Branley
Illustrations copyright © 1989 by E. P. Dutton

Library of Congress Cataloging-in-Publication Data

Branley, Franklyn Mansfield, date
  Mysteries of planet earth.

  (Mysteries of the universe series)
  Bibliography: p.
  Includes index.
  1. Earth—Popular works. 2. Astronomy—Popular
works. I. Bensusen, Sally J. II. Title. III. Series:
Branley, Franklyn Mansfield, date Mysteries of the
universe series.
  QB631.2.B72 1989 525 88-31076
  ISBN 0-525-67278-8

Published in the United States by
E. P. Dutton, New York, N.Y.,
a division of NAL Penguin Inc.

Published simultaneously in Canada by
Fitzhenry & Whiteside Limited, Toronto

Editor: Virginia Buckley   Designer: Riki Levinson

Printed in the U.S.A.   First Edition
10 9 8 7 6 5 4 3 2 1

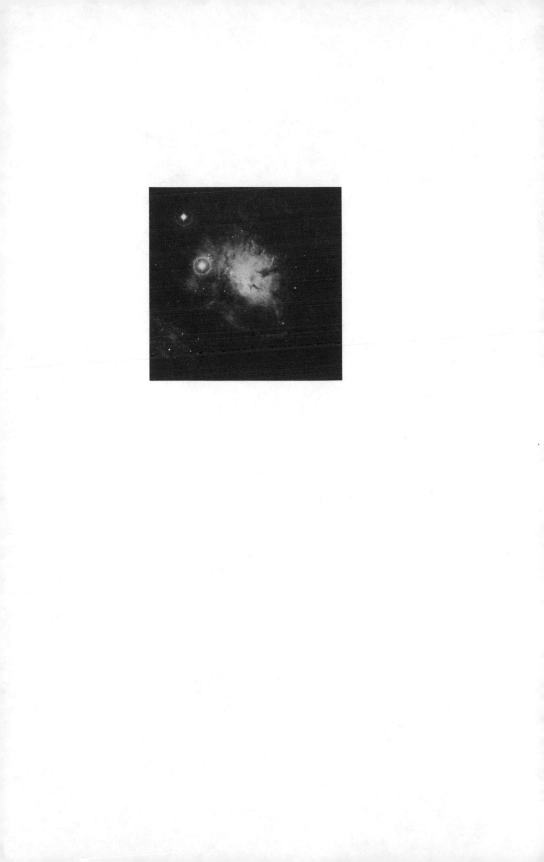

CONTENTS

1 MYSTERIES LEAD TO MORE MYSTERIES

We are all curious about ourselves and our surroundings. Mysteries about the solar system, stars, and universe interest us. So also do mysteries about planet Earth.

Earth is a medium-size planet; four of the planets of the solar system are larger than it, four are smaller. Among the planets, the mass of Earth—the amount of material it contains—is also in the middle. The mass of Earth is 6×10^{24} kilograms (6×10^{21} tons). Powers of ten is a shorthand method for writing large numbers; one hundred is 1×10^{2}, and one thousand is 1×10^{3}, so 6×10^{21} turns out to be a large number indeed—6 000 000 000 000 000 000 000, which is 6 sextillion tons. It is difficult to imagine such a number, but this example might help. A pile of $1000 bills 4 inches high would be a million dollars. To make a trillion, the pile would have to be 63 miles high. Six sextillion is a billion times greater.

There are many mysteries about our planet that keep us guessing. We wonder why the sea is salty. An early explanation was that rivers and streams dissolved salts out of rocks and deposited them in the oceans. That is part of the answer, but there is more.

– And why should Earth be the only planet that has life on it? That is a mystery that has puzzled many people for a long time. It is far from being solved.

What will eventually happen to Earth? Will it freeze solid, or will it become hot enough to change to gases? Perhaps neither will happen. It may go on and on forever. That is another mystery to explore.

People like to have beginnings and endings for everything. So to many of them, the most basic of all the riddles of our planet is how and when it first appeared. Let's take a look at that mystery and see how scientists have attempted to solve it.

2 THE BEGINNING OF EARTH

How old is Earth?

The Egyptians built the pyramids thousands of years ago. Long before that, the Babylonians and Chaldeans flourished in the Tigris River valley. It seems that Earth has been here forever. But how long is forever?

Several attempts have been made to answer that question. In 1642, an Englishman by the name of John Lightfoot pronounced that the beginning of Earth was at 9 A.M., September 17, 3928 B.C. He may have based his calculation on a study of the generations of families in the Old Testament. A few years later that's what Archbishop James Ussher of Ireland did. He studied the families of the Bible and then wrote:

> In the beginning God created heaven and Earth [Gen. 1:1], which beginning of time, according to our chronologie, fell upon the entrance of night preceding the twenty-third day of the Julian calendar, 710.

The Julian calendar is a special one used by astronomers. Some fifty years later, Bishop Lloyd of England changed the date to 4064 B.C., using the ordinary calendar. For over a hundred years that date was accepted as the beginning of Earth.

But we now know that the world is much older than that. It is true that written history goes back only about five thousand years, to the Chaldeans. Yet scientists tell us that modern man appeared about a million years ago. And ancient man was here a million or more years before that. It is now believed that the entire history of humans, both modern and ancient, is only a moment in the history of Earth. The age of our planet seems to be about 4.6 billion years. We accept this figure because of theories about the Sun, which will be discussed later, and because of the ability to radioactively date rocks.

What is radioactive dating?

To understand how dating works, think of an ice cube that weighs one kilogram. Suppose in one hour exactly half the ice cube melted away. Then you would have half a kilogram. In two hours you would have a quarter; in three hours, an eighth; in four hours, a sixteenth; and so on. If you came across an ice cube that weighed one-eighth a kilogram, you would immediately know that the cube was three hours old. In radioactive dating, atoms take the place of the ice cubes in our model.

Certain atoms are radioactive—they give off energy and particles. As they do this, the atoms change from one element to another. They keep changing until the atoms produced are stable, that is, until they are not radioactive. Radioactive atoms change to stable atoms at a steady rate called the half-life of the element. In our ice example, the half-life of the cube was one hour—in one hour, half the ice had changed to water. The half-life of uranium 235, a radioactive element, is 710 million years. In that many years, half the uranium 235 will have changed to lead. So, the age of a rock can be figured out by determining how much lead and uranium 235 there is in the sample. When uranium first formed, all the atoms in a given rock were uranium, no lead was present. After a billion years, twelve of every one hundred atoms had become lead; in two billion years, twenty-two had become lead; and so on. Helium also formed, but much of that escaped, so it is not usually used in the calculation. Here is what happens:

Billions of years	Number of atoms in a sample		
	Uranium	Lead	Helium
0	100	0	0
1	86	12	2
2	75	22	3
3	65	30	5
4 (half-life)	50	43	7
Finally	00	86	14

The scientist has to find the ratio of lead to uranium. Once this is known, the age of the sample can be determined. For example:

When ratio of lead to uranium is	then	age of sample in millions of years is
.080		500
.166		1000
.360		2000

In figuring the ages of rocks, other radioactive elements such as radium, thorium, and rubidium can also be used.

The most ancient rocks found on Earth are 3.8 billion years old. Most are much younger. Rocks far below the surface cannot be reached, so their ages are unknown. However, it is believed they are older than the surface rocks.

Moon rocks are older than those on Earth. Rocks on the lunar surface are just as they were when first laid down. There has been no erosion or transportation of them as there has been with Earth rocks. Some moon rocks are 4.6 billion years old. We believe that Earth's interior rocks would also be that old, since the Moon and Earth were very likely formed at the same time.

Rocks on the surface of the Moon are much older than rocks on Earth's surface. NASA

Meteorites are also very old, and they are unchanged because there has been little, if any, erosion of them. When they are dated, the ages of meteorites are often about 4.6 billion years. It is believed they were also formed about the same time Earth came into existence.

˟All the ages of moon rocks, meteorites, and earth rocks do not fall at exactly 4.6 billion years. Many are younger. But there is enough agreement to conclude that Earth, and perhaps the entire solar system, is about 4.6 billion years old.

How did Earth begin?

Earth represents a very small part of the solar system. In fact, 99.86 percent of the mass of the system is in the Sun. Earth and all the other planets, the satellites, asteroids, meteoroids, comets, and interplanetary dust altogether make up the difference—only 14 hundredths of 1 percent. Among the planets, Earth's mass is minor; the total mass of all the other planets combined, mostly from Jupiter, is almost five hundred times greater than that of Earth.

Since the Sun is such a major part of the solar system, attempts to solve the mystery of Earth's origin must focus on the Sun.

The Sun is a secondhand star, which means it is made of used materials. We know this because, in addition to hydrogen and helium, which are the only ingredients of the oldest stars, the Sun also contains carbon, zinc, iron, and some sixty other elements. Much of the material in it was made in very hot stars that exploded and threw the substances into space. By comparing the Sun with a variety of stars, and by creating theories about what goes on during the life histories of stars, astronomers have determined that the Sun is five or six billion years old. That makes it young, for the first stars formed some ten or twelve billion years ago out of original hydrogen and helium.

The Lagoon Nebula in Sagittarius. The Sun probably began as a similar nebula. HALE OBSERVATORIES

Star formation continues today. In our galaxy, there are many nebulas—clouds of gaseous hydrogen, helium, and other elements. In some of these nebulas, there are dark patches where the materials are packed together more densely and are continuing to grow. The masses of them—the amount of material they contain—are very large. In many cases the dark patches contain enough material to make a Sun or even a larger star. Distances between patches are often similar to the distances between the Sun and its neighbor stars.

Very likely these dark patches are proto-stars, stars in early stages of formation. The gases will continue to pack together and will eventually become massive enough to collapse into a dense sphere. After eons, the collapse will cause the system to heat up to a level high enough for nuclear reactions to occur. The heat generated by fusion will create outward pressure that will prevent further collapse. The two forces will balance each other, and a star will be born.

It is thought that the Sun originated in a similar fashion. And, very likely, Earth and the other planets are made of its leftover materials—waste products of Sun formation. Steps in the process may have been these: The Sun may have evolved out of a spherical mass of gases, mostly hydrogen and helium, that had a diameter of 15 billion kilometers. The gases first

The Sun formed out of gases and also out of material created in older stars that formed and exploded long ago.

packed together, then collapsed into a formation only a fraction of their original volume. As collapse continued, the spherical system rotated, causing ·it to become elongated and flattened. It became a disk 9.5 million kilometers across, with a bulging central region.

— Because of its great mass, the central bulge attracted most of the material. It became the Sun. The remaining gases churned and spun about the central mass. Here and there, clumps formed in the gases. Most broke up, but some few persisted. Because of their greater masses, they pulled in more and more of the gases. Each system held together and became a protoplanet. More gases collected in the clumps, and each finally collapsed. Since there was not enough mass for any of the clumps to become stars, they became planets. Their orbits about the central formation, the Sun, changed from a flat ellipse to shapes more nearly circular.

Ninety-nine percent of the Sun is hydrogen and helium; all the other elements in it amount to only one percent. So it was with the protoplanets. At one time, Earth contained mostly hydrogen and helium, with traces of many other elements. Gradually, compounds of hydrogen formed—water (H_2O), methane (CH_4), and ammonia (NH_3). The temperature was low enough for the compounds to freeze into crystals. Denser materials such as iron and nickel were pulled into the central core. Lighter materials formed a crust, and surrounding all was an envelope of hydrogen and helium.

The young Sun was unstable. Explosions occurred occasionally, and these explosions blew out clouds of particles. They were energetic enough to blow away most of the gases surrounding Earth, and sudden increases in solar energy evaporated materials from the crust as well. Earth's atmosphere, and its water, appeared much later. In large part, they originated under Earth's crust and were carried to the surface by planet-wide volcanic eruptions that lasted for millenniums.

Earth is sometimes called the water planet. Much of it is always cloud covered. NASA

This is a possible answer to the question of Earth's beginning. Maybe this is the way it all happened. No one would say the mystery is solved, however; for although a lot has been learned about the planet, there is much unknown. An equally challenging riddle is how and when life appeared.

3 LIFE ON PLANET EARTH

As far as has been explored, no life has been found beyond Earth: not on the Moon, Venus, Mars, or any of the other planets or their satellites—not anywhere in the solar system. Nor do we have any evidence of life in the vast regions beyond. Our planet is the only place in the entire universe where life is known to exist. Many believe there are millions of other planets out among the stars. And they are convinced that life of some kind has appeared on a great many of those planets. They may be right. However, at this time it must be assumed that Earth is the only planet that supports living plants and animals. An important mystery is how and when life appeared.

When did life appear?

No one can say. Fossils are the only evidence we have of ancient life. The earliest fossils go back two or perhaps three billion years. Some people believe there are even older remains of ancient plants. But the fact is, the continuous fossil record

Earth is roughly 4.6 billion years old. Life probably appeared ▶
over a billion years ago, but the continuous fossil record goes
back only 500 million years.

Geologic Time

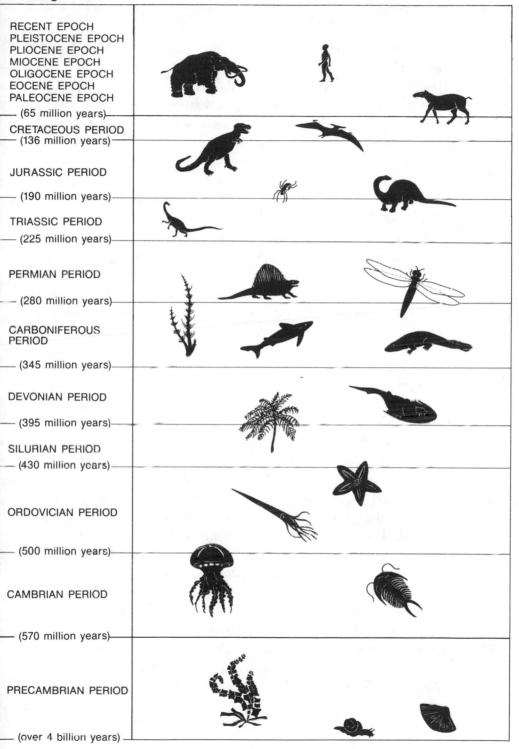

RECENT EPOCH
PLEISTOCENE EPOCH
PLIOCENE EPOCH
MIOCENE EPOCH
OLIGOCENE EPOCH
EOCENE EPOCH
PALEOCENE EPOCH
— (65 million years)—
CRETACEOUS PERIOD
— (136 million years)—

JURASSIC PERIOD

— (190 million years)—

TRIASSIC PERIOD

— (225 million years)—

PERMIAN PERIOD

— (280 million years)—

CARBONIFEROUS
PERIOD

— (345 million years)—

DEVONIAN PERIOD

— (395 million years)—

SILURIAN PERIOD
— (430 million years)—

ORDOVICIAN PERIOD

— (500 million years)—

CAMBRIAN PERIOD

— (570 million years)—

PRECAMBRIAN PERIOD

— (over 4 billion years) —

starts much later; it begins only 500 million years ago. There are traces of carbon in older rocks, and the carbon may have been associated with living organisms. But remains of earlier life are scarce, because the first creatures were soft-bodied. When they died and became incorporated into rocks, no structure remained, and so fossils are not clearly defined.

Maybe life appeared two or three billion years ago. When it did, Earth was far different than it is today. For one thing, there were no continents as we know them, only sections of solid material floating on a hot, frothing sea. The atmosphere was largely methane and ammonia, quite different from the nitrogen and oxygen that now compose it. Very likely, powerful lightning discharges ripped through the atmosphere. And, just as lightning causes chemical changes in the atmosphere today, it changed the structure of molecules in the ancient atmosphere.

Methane, ammonia, and water are common planetary substances also found in interplanetary space. All are compounds of hydrogen, which is the basic ingredient of the entire universe. A few years ago, scientists who were pursuing the mystery of the appearance of life reasoned that life may have been formed from these hydrogen compounds as lightning activated them. To test the idea, they set up an experiment. Ammonia, methane, and hydrogen were introduced into a steam-filled globe. Energetic electric sparks (lightning) passed through the mixture. When this was done, amino acids formed. These acids are the building blocks of proteins, and proteins are substances essential to life.

Such reactions may have occurred on the early planet. Most of the amino acids broke down and disappeared. But at some time, certain of these materials may have fallen into the sea, where they survived. In some manner, certain of the molecules were able to grow. More importantly, they developed the ability to produce other molecules—they could grow and they could also reproduce. Eventually molecules bunched together to form a primitive organism, perhaps a simple plant such as a bacterium. After millions of years, more complex plants appeared, those that could use the energy of the Sun along with carbon dioxide to produce starches. These were probably algae, plants of the sea, which created the oldest known fossils.

Unless more specialized life forms developed, life would have ended with the algae. Eventually one-celled organisms called protozoans appeared, and with them, the mechanisms of living were complete—movement, digestion of food, and sexual reproduction. The time gap between the creation of an organic molecule and the appearance of a protozoan was interminable. It was at least as long, and as great a step, as that between those early protozoans and the appearance of man. Much later, when clusters of single-celled organisms appeared, and with them the separation of functions, certain cells had special tasks to perform. The complexity of organisms grew, no doubt taking millions of years to make major strides. Much later, animals with backbones, vertebrates, appeared. The stage was set for the various life forms that have evolved during the past several million years.

Biologists say that early stages such as these might have occurred. They appear possible, according to present-day knowledge. A few of the steps can be duplicated, such as the production of amino acids. But the manner in which these basic molecules became living forms remains an intriguing riddle.

Is there life beyond Earth?

Another major mystery connected with life on Earth is the question of life's existence elsewhere in the universe. If life appeared on Earth in the manner suggested above, then it would seem that among the requirements for life are heat, violent electric discharges, and the presence of certain chemicals such as ammonia, methane, hydrogen, and water.

Jupiter has all these conditions. Some people believe amino acids are being produced in the atmosphere of that planet. If they are, the molecules break down and do not survive. An essential step in the process may be the placing of the molecules in temperate water. This is a condition that does not exist on Jupiter. Eventually seas may form there, but presently no one believes that living organisms have appeared on the giant planet. Nor have they appeared anywhere else in the solar system.

In our galaxy there are at least 200 billion stars. It is believed that among them there must be many that have planets going around them. Among those planets, there must be many that have evolved the same way Earth has. Events that have occurred here may have also taken place at those alien locations. Life may be a common condition on these far-off worlds. Eventually we may develop ways to find out for sure, to answer a significant question.

Space telescopes may be able to measure slight back-and-forth motions of certain stars. If so, those movements would imply that planets going around the stars are causing the oscillations. In 1983, the Infrared Astronomical Satellite (IRAS) discovered a cloud of cool, solid objects around Vega, the brightest star in Lyra, a summer constellation. The objects are small, though it seems some are large enough to be called planets.

Vega is a young star, about a third the age of the Sun. Therefore, some observers believe IRAS discovered protoplanets—planets in the process of formation. If so, it is logical to expect that similar events have occurred around other, older stars. They may possess developed planets. All that is needed are instruments sensitive enough to discover their presence.

Our galaxy of billions of stars is only one of the billions of galaxies that make up the universe. And each of those galaxies contains stars, in some cases many more than the 200 billion in our own galaxy.

One can easily suppose that somewhere among those thousands of trillions of stars there are many that have clouds of cool objects around them, just as Vega has. Some of them might even have planets with living creatures on them.

The mystery of how life began on Earth then becomes the mystery of life in the universe. We wonder about conditions on far-off alien worlds. Do they have mountains and valleys, continents and oceans? If so, are the seas as large as ours? Do they flourish with life?

IRAS (Infrared Astronomical Satellite)   NASA

THE SALTY SEA

Taste it, and you certainly know that seawater is salty. Ordinary salt, which is sodium chloride, accounts for much of the taste. But there are lots of other substances in seawater. One can find Epsom salts, Glauber's salt, calcium chloride, calcium carbonate, and gypsum. Seventy-three elements, among them zinc, tin, lead, gold, silver, lithium, carbon, and bromine, have been detected in seawater. Where they all come from has been a major mystery.

Do sea salts come from the land?

In the early 1700s, people learned that streams which flowed into seas carried dissolved minerals. It was believed that these were the minerals that made the sea salty. In 1715, Edmund Halley, the Englishman after whom Halley's comet is named, suggested a way to find the age of the oceans and Earth. He said all one needed to do was calculate how much salt there was in the ocean and how much goes into the ocean each year. Divide one into the other, and that is the age of the ocean. About two hundred years later, an attempt was made to do this. By that process, the age of Earth turned out to be 90 million years. We now know it is a lot older, so there must be some other way that the ocean becomes salty.

According to a Norwegian legend, there is a huge salt mill somewhere at the bottom of the sea. The mill grinds away, continually adding salt, so the sea is kept salty. It turns out that there may be a lot of truth to the legend, although the salt mill is quite different from the hand-operated one of the legend.

Do sea salts come from beneath the sea?

The sea bottom is not smooth and unbroken. There are cracks, or rifts, as they are called, sometimes extending for thousands of miles. These are openings in the crust of the Earth that widen by several centimeters every year. As they do, pressure on water trapped in the crustal rocks is released, and the water comes out of them. It is "new" water, and it contains salts and other substances including chlorine, bromine, and iodine. These three elements are fairly abundant in seawater. But they are not found in Earth's surface rocks, so of course they could not have come from them.

New water is also added by volcanoes; perhaps these are the "salt mills" of the legend. In certain locations, volcanoes are under the sea. On occasion they erupt violently, sometimes releasing enough lava to build new islands. All of them release elements into the sea. Volcanoes on land also give off bromine, iodine, and other materials, many of which fall into the sea.

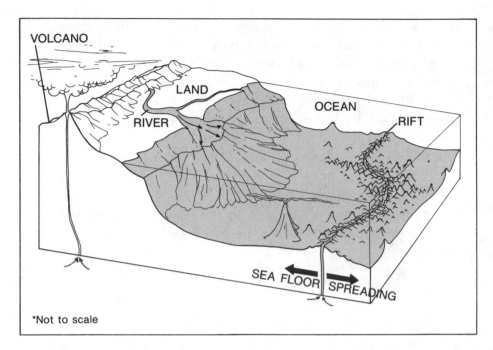

VOLCANO
LAND
RIVER
OCEAN
RIFT
SEA FLOOR SPREADING
*Not to scale

Rivers carry salts into the sea. Also, new salts are added as water emerges through rifts in Earth's crust and in the eruptions of volcanoes.

Does the sea increase in saltiness?

Although salts are carried to the sea by streams and are added to new water, it is believed that the saltiness of the sea has not changed very much for at least 200 million years. Therefore, there must be ways of removing some of the salts or of changing them in some manner. Sea plants and animals do change the salts. Certain algae take in iodine, for example, and many organisms take in calcium carbonate to make their shells.

At the same time, salts leave the sea and go into the atmosphere. Wind and wave action make a fine sea spray, and water droplets containing salt are picked up by the wind blowing across it. Salt becomes the solid particles upon which water vapor in the atmosphere condenses—raindrops grow around salt particles. When it rains, the salt is carried to Earth. Raindrops account for more than 90 percent of the chloride and 50 percent of the sodium that is carried to the sea by rivers and streams.

What is the carbon dioxide cycle?

In the ocean, some chemical reactions change dissolved substances into solids that settle out. This action, together with organic reactions such as those in algae, keeps the composition of seawater essentially the same, year in and year out. Fortunately, the sea also removes carbon dioxide from our atmosphere.

Carbon dioxide is essential to the growth of green plants. We need a small amount of it because it stimulates our breathing. But too much carbon dioxide would be poisonous. It would also cause a world-wide disaster because of the resulting temperature changes. Carbon dioxide might serve as a blanket preventing the loss of heat from Earth. This means average temperature of the planet might increase two or three degrees, enough to cause the ice caps of Greenland and Antarctica to melt, raising sea level enough to cause catastrophic floods on every continent.

In the past century, the amount of carbon dioxide in the atmosphere has increased from 290 parts per million to 320. According to most scientists, that figure should be 350. Apparently seawater has removed the excess. The carbon dioxide originally leaves the atmosphere and dissolves in the upper layers of the sea. Over periods of thousands of years, it becomes mixed into the deeper layers. But the process is very slow. It is so slow, it is possible the carbon dioxide content of the atmosphere will reach 480 parts per million by the end of this century. That may be enough to cause the melting of ice caps mentioned above. Since we cannot accelerate the take-up of carbon dioxide by seawater, it is important that we decrease the amount we put into the air. We must decrease the burning of fossil fuels, because that is the main source of the increased carbon dioxide. And forests must not be destroyed, for trees also take carbon dioxide out of the air.

On Earth, there are delicate balances among plants, the atmosphere, and the ocean. Should ocean water be greatly changed by oil spills or the dumping of sewage, garbage, and chemical wastes, the processes that keep these balances even would be interrupted. Results could be disastrous not only for the plants and animals in the oceans but also for those that live on land. The oceans keep us alive, so it is essential they not be polluted or otherwise changed by people.

5 TEMPERATURE OF EARTH

Day and night, year after year, Earth's temperature remains about the same. But this is not true of some of the other planets. During its day, Mercury reaches 350° Celsius (C), but at night the planet cools sharply to 185° below zero. Parts of Mars get quite warm in direct sunlight, but they become freezing cold right after sunset. The temperature of Venus does not change; it holds at 460°, the hottest overall of the nine planets. Temperatures of the outer planets do not vary much either. The upper clouds of the big, gaseous planets are always cold, as is Pluto. Below the clouds, the gaseous planets are much warmer, perhaps as hot as 20 000° in certain locations. Nonetheless, the overall temperatures of these planets are still cooler than that of Venus.

Earth is a steady-temperature planet. Earth has day/night changes in temperature, and has changes from season to season. But these are local or regional variations. The temperature of the planet as a whole holds at a steady 14°C. That is the temperature that aliens in a spaceship out beyond Earth would record.

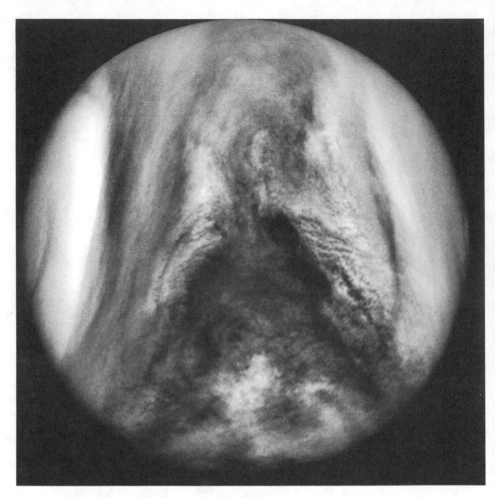

Venus is the hottest of all the planets. NASA

Has Earth's temperature changed?

Parts of the Earth have gone through long-lasting changes. We know this because fossil plants have been found in regions that are now ice covered. Also, fossils of mammoths that thrived in Arctic conditions have been found in places now much warmer, such as the central part of our country.

Many scientists believe that 65 million years ago Earth cooled enough to kill lush tropical plants—the food of many dinosaurs. Dinosaurs probably disappeared from the planet abruptly because, for some reason, Earth cooled so that large parts of it could no longer support the growth of tropical plants. Fortunately, not all plants and animals were destroyed, and so life continues to flourish though there have been changes in the varieties that dominate the planet.

When Earth formed, about 4.6 billion years ago, the Sun was a lot cooler than it is now. It remained cool for a long time, cold enough so that the oceans should have frozen. But they did not. They couldn't have, because fossils of ocean life believed to be 3 billion years old have been found. Why the Earth did not freeze is a mystery that has been explored by many scientists.

Perhaps, they suggest, the atmosphere of ancient Earth had a lot more carbon dioxide than it has now. Perhaps there was enough to trap solar heat, keep it from escaping, and so keep Earth warm. If that was so, why didn't Earth continue to get hotter and hotter? That is another riddle.

Possibly, some 2 billion years ago, algae in the seas began taking carbon dioxide out of the air and using it to make other compounds by photosynthesis, the food-making process of green plants. Since the amount of carbon dioxide was reduced, heat could escape and so the temperature of Earth did not build up.

Over billions of years, the Sun's temperature has increased. At the same time, green plants have flourished, and so they have removed carbon dioxide. Heat loss has come to equal heat gain, and so the temperature of the planet has stabilized.

Presently the amount of carbon dioxide is increasing partly because of the clearing of forests. But a more important cause of the increase is the burning of fuels, especially coal and oil. According to some scientists, in the next century there may be enough atmospheric carbon dioxide to cause Earth's temperature to rise several degrees and cause the melting mentioned earlier. The increased temperature would also cause severe changes in the world's weather systems. Regions now lacking rainfall might become rich farmland, and areas now producing crops might become wastelands.

How is Earth heated?

All the planets are heated by the Sun. That star is the source of most of the energy in the solar system. Since this is so, one would expect that planets nearest the Sun would be the hottest, and the more distant ones, the coldest. Generally that is true, but other factors also affect temperature.

Atmosphere is one of these factors. Venus has a dense, opaque atmosphere made mostly of carbon dioxide. The gas is a blanket that prevents the passage of heat. Sunlight streaming into the planet has short waves that can go through carbon dioxide. Once that radiation reaches the surface of Venus, it changes to long-wave heat energy. These waves cannot penetrate carbon dioxide, so the heat is trapped. The heat has built up to a temperature of 460°C, and it holds there day after day, year after year.

Jupiter and Saturn are far from the Sun, so one would expect them to be cold. And they are. However, the planets are a lot warmer than they should be with the Sun as their only source of energy.

Why the planets should be warmer than expected is a mystery, although solutions have been suggested. Perhaps radioactive materials lie deep within the planets. If so, they would give off heat, and would do so for millenniums. Others say that the planets are still cooling off, releasing heat that was generated at the time they were formed. Another theory holds that the heat is generated as helium, which abounds in the atmosphere, falling through the lighter hydrogen of the atmo-

Saturn is cool, as are all the major planets. NASA

sphere. Collisions of the helium and hydrogen molecules might be enough to generate large amounts of heat.

Most of Earth's heat comes from the Sun. Smaller amounts come from the breakdown of radioactive elements in Earth's crust and from interior heat caused by the packing of Earth's mass.

Earth is roughly 150 million kilometers from the Sun. That

distance is perfect, for Earth receives just enough solar energy to maintain life-supporting temperatures. Were it to move slightly closer, the oceans would gradually become warmer. Evaporation would increase and the atmosphere would become overladen with water vapor. The vapor would act as a mirror, reflecting some sunlight into space but more effectively reflecting longer-wave heat back to Earth. This would raise temperature even higher. Eventually the oceans would be gone. Rocks in the crust would bake, releasing tremendous amounts of carbon dioxide. Since plants would have perished, there would be no way to remove the carbon dioxide. The atmosphere would become a very effective heat holder. Earth's temperature would soar by hundreds of degrees.

If Earth were slightly farther from the Sun, the effects would also be fatal. A small drop in annual temperature would cause a build-up of glaciers in high mountains and in northern and southern latitudes. After a few centuries, the glaciers would push into the temperate regions, squeezing from the far north and south toward the warmer central areas of the planet. This would accelerate the cooling of the oceans. As ice cover increased, more sunlight would be reflected from the ice, which would act as a mirror, and cooling would be speeded. Year after year, ice would creep toward the equator. Earth would become ice-covered, a cold and lifeless desert.

Earth's location is just right for its plants and animals. It is difficult to conceive how Earth could ever move farther from the Sun or closer to it. So it seems that the present favorable conditions on our planet should continue. However, as will be discovered in the last chapter, the scenario for Earth in the distant future is not all that pleasant.

EARTH'S MAGNETISM

Earth behaves as though it were a huge magnet with the force centered at the north and south magnetic poles. At the present time, the north-seeking end of a compass needle points toward the north magnetic pole, a region about 20 degrees from the north geographic pole. But it has not always been so. In fact, during the past 3.5 million years, the magnetic poles have switched north to south and south to north at least nine times. And very likely they switched many times more during the earlier history of the planet. That is a mystery that interests scientists.

How far does Earth's magnetism extend?

When probes were first sent out beyond our atmosphere, they found that Earth's magnetic field extends some 100 000 kilometers into space. It captures some of the charged particles, mostly protons and electrons, that are ejected from the Sun in the solar wind. These particles then become arranged in belts. The belts are doughnut-like regions of charged parti-

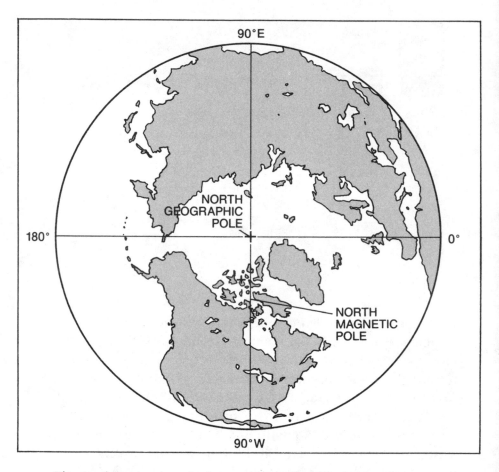

The north magnetic pole does not coincide with the north geographic pole. The magnetic pole is located at north latitude 70 and west latitude 100.

cles that are flattened on the Sun side of Earth and trail out on the side away from the Sun. Most of the solar particles are not captured; they are deflected by the magnetosphere and so flow around and stream past the planet.

The solution to the mystery of how Earth's magnetism is produced is tied closely to electricity. If we discover why Earth has electricity, we will discover why it is magnetic.

How are magnetism and electricity related?

If you have an electric current, you also have magnetism. And under certain conditions, if there is magnetism, there is also an electric current. A wire conducting electricity is magnetic. If a piece of wire is wound around a nail and the ends of the wire are fastened to a battery, the nail becomes a magnet. The coil and the nail serve to concentrate the field.

If you start with a magnet, electricity can be generated. Make a coil of wire, and move a magnet in and out of the coil. That is all you have to do to generate a current. The bigger the coil and the stronger the magnet, the greater the current.

Since Earth has a magnetic field, it follows that there must be currents of electricity within the planet. Scientists have explored how and why that electric current is generated.

When a disk is turned over a coil of wire, an electric current is generated.

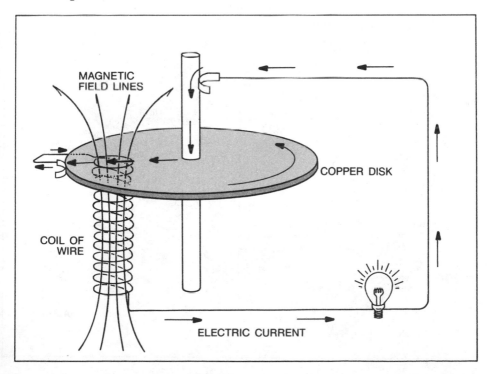

What is a dynamo?

Electricity may be generated in many different ways: with solar-electric cells; by chemical action, as in batteries; and by what is called the dynamo effect. The moving-magnet idea mentioned above is a kind of dynamo. Another is one that was developed in the early nineteenth century by Michael Faraday, an English scientist. He spun a copper disk above the end of a bar magnet. When the disk was moving, an electric current was generated in it. Instead of a bar magnet, an electric coil could be used because, as you remember, a magnetic field surrounds a current-carrying wire. When a part of the electricity is fed into the coil, the system becomes self-sustaining—one part feeds the other.

The idea is sound enough. However, not much electricity is made. Better conductors would improve the situation. Also, more electricity is obtained when the disk is spun very fast. Or, if the disk could be made larger, there would be more electricity. A disk several miles in diameter would generate electricity even if the disk spun slowly. A disk as large as Earth would be effective even if it hardly moved.

Michael Faraday's experiment

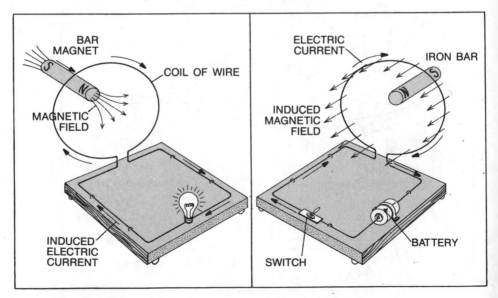

The dynamo idea is probably at least part of the answer to the question of Earth's magnetism. Geologists say that inside Earth there is a fluid rock and metallic layer. Since it is liquid, or semi-liquid, this layer can move past solid portions of Earth's interior. The fluid contains metals, and therefore it is a conductor of electricity just as the copper disk is in Faraday's dynamo. Electricity in the liquid may be generated by chemical processes. A difference of one volt between the poles and the equator would be more than enough to produce Earth's magnetism. The electricity generates magnetism, and the magnetism enhances the electricity-generating process; the system becomes self-sustaining.

Scientists believe that the liquid section moves roughly one millimeter a second. It is not clear where the energy for this motion comes from; convection currents caused by temperature and density differences may account for it. However, very little energy is needed to set up the motion.

Small spinning areas—eddies—are produced as the dynamo process continues. These cause slight variations that have been noted in the general magnetic field of the planet.

Do other planets have magnetism?

If the theory about Earth's magnetism is correct, it would mean that other bodies that have liquid cores or layers should also have magnetic fields. Those without underlying liquid zones would lack magnetic fields. As far as we know, that appears to be so. The Moon has no magnetic field. Moonquakes tell us that the Moon is a solid body. The lack of a field confirms the theory. Mars and Venus have no magnetic fields, which means they may lack liquid interior sections. Further investigations will hopefully be made with instruments that measure quakes on those planets. When records of the quakes are studied, scientists can map out the various regions of the planets and determine if any of them are liquid.

The major planets appear to have magnetic fields, even though their central solid cores are very small. However, in those planets, the gases in underlying shells are highly compressed, so much so that they behave as liquids and so may produce the dynamo effect.

Whatever the reason for Earth's magnetism may be, it appears to be related to a liquid region and to the planet's rotation.

7 ROTATION AND OTHER MOTIONS OF EARTH

Rotation is a motion found throughout the solar system. There are objects that rotate rapidly—Jupiter makes a turn in about 10 hours—while others rotate slowly, Venus in about 244 days. Like all other motions, rotation, once started, continues forever unless some force acts to stop it. How did these motions get started?

Why do planets rotate?

The search for the answer goes back to the early history of the planets. It is believed Earth formed out of the same gaseous cloud that gave birth to the Sun and the other planets. The particles were in violent motion, colliding and bouncing off one another. Eventually, several particles collided at just the right velocity and direction to cause them to clump together. Such a cluster had great enough mass to attract other particles. The cluster grew. As the particles built up, their motions caused the cluster to spin around—to rotate. Nearby masses affected the rotations of each other. For example, the Moon affected Earth's rotation then, and it does so today.

How does rotation affect nearby bodies?

The Moon raises tides in Earth's oceans as well as in its solid portions. As Earth turns past the Moon, the tidal attraction—Moon's gravitation—acts as a brake, slowing down the rotation a thousandth of a second in a hundred years.

In a similar manner, Earth's gravitation acts upon the Moon's rotation. Because of Earth's greater mass, its gravitational attraction is strong enough to cause large land tides on the Moon. Over millions of years, the tidal drag has slowed the rotation so that, relative to the Earth, the Moon does not rotate. Another way of saying this is that the same face of the Moon is always toward the Earth. This has caused that face to bulge toward the Earth.

What is the Earth clock?

Because of its rotation, Earth can be used as a clock. There are slight variations in the time necessary to complete a rotation, caused by the expansion and contraction of the planet and also by the shifting of ice and snow masses on the surface. But for the most part Earth rotates at a fixed rate, and so it is a clock. One day is 23 hours, 56 minutes, 4.091 seconds long—the time required for Earth to make a single rotation as measured by a distant star. It is a sidereal, or star, day. In such a brief time, a star does not move noticeably, so it is a fixed point in the sky.

More accurate clocks, such as those that use the frequency of electromagnetic radiation given off by atoms or molecules, enabled scientists to find the small variations in the Earth clock. Atomic clocks keep time to an accuracy of one second in 30 000 years. That is more accurate than Earth's rotation.

How long do planets take to revolve?

Like rotation, revolution is a condition that prevails throughout the solar system; in fact, throughout the universe. As objects spin, they also go around other objects—they revolve. Stars go around other stars, satellites go around planets, planets go around the Sun, and so on.

To go around the Sun, Earth takes one year to complete a journey of about 943 million kilometers. Its average velocity is 105 thousand kilometers an hour—29.6 kilometers a second. Planets closer to the Sun move at faster velocities while those farther away move more slowly.

Planet	Velocity in Orbit (km per sec)	Revolution Time (in days or years)
Mercury	47.5	88.00 d
Venus	34.9	224.70 d
Earth	29.6	365.26 d
Mars	24.0	687.00 d
Jupiter	12.9	11.86 y
Saturn	9.6	29.46 y
Uranus	6.7	84.01 y
Neptune	5.4	164.80 y
Pluto	4.7	247.70 y

The path or orbit that Earth follows around the Sun is a fat ellipse—it is not far from being a circle. However, since the orbit is elliptical, the distance between Earth and the Sun varies. During winter in the northern hemisphere, Earth is closest to the Sun, some 146 million kilometers away. Earth is at the greatest distance in July, when Earth and the Sun are separated by 151 million kilometers.

Variation in distance is not the main factor affecting Earth's seasons. Rather, it is the tilt of Earth's axis. During winter, Earth's northern half is tilted away from the Sun, so that half receives much less heat.

What is Earth's barycenter?

To be accurate, we have to say that two bodies do not revolve around each other. Rather, they revolve around their barycenter—the center of mass in the two-body system. As an example, think of a seesaw. The people on either end may have different masses, yet they pivot around their balance point. If one person's mass is much greater than that of the other, the pivot will be close to the greater mass. In a similar way, Earth and the Moon pivot around their center of mass, which is very close to Earth. In fact, it is inside the planet— about 1600 kilometers below the surface.

Think of the pivot of the seesaw moving along as the people swing around it. Sometimes the greater mass would be ahead of the pivot and at other times behind it. Similarly, as the Earth-Moon system revolves around the Sun, Earth is sometimes ahead of its geometric center and at other times behind it. The amount can be determined by careful measurements of the orbital positions of Mars. The planet appears a bit farther along in its orbit than it should be and then a bit behind its predicted position. The changes are caused by Earth's being a bit ahead or behind its center. The variations in the positions of Mars indicate that the location of the barycenter is as indicated above—1600 kilometers below Earth's surface.

The barycenter is the center of mass of the Earth-Moon system.

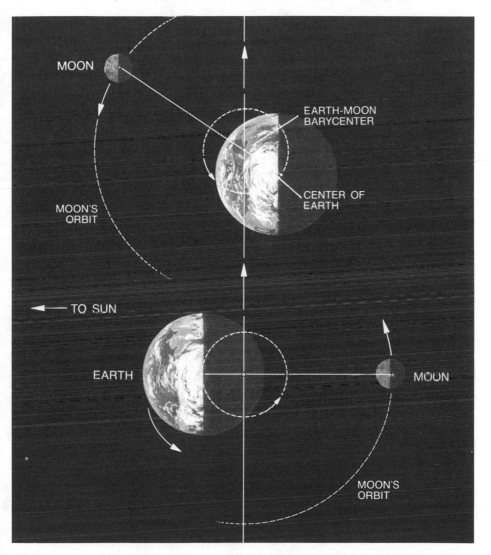

Why do planets revolve?

After scientists discovered that the Moon went around Earth and the planets went around the Sun, they wondered how this could be. What held these bodies in space? What kept them moving? Why didn't the Moon fall to Earth, and why didn't the planets fall into the Sun? The mysteries were unsolved until Sir Isaac Newton (1642–1727), the famous English scientist, proposed the solution.

Motion is a constant. All objects in the universe—from stars and galaxies to atoms and electrons—are in motion. Also, all objects have mass and so they pull on other masses. If one mass is much greater than another, the less massive object must move very fast to avoid being pulled into the larger one.

Consider the Moon and why and how it remains in orbit around the Earth.

The Moon stays in orbit because it is always falling toward Earth. That sounds impossible, but it is true. Each second the Moon falls about a millimeter toward Earth. But it does not fall closer to Earth, because at the same time the Moon is moving forward 1020 meters a second. Therefore, the Moon falls toward Earth in a curve. And the curve is such that it carries the Moon around Earth.

Newton explained the mystery by supposing a gun were mounted high above Earth, aimed along a line tangent to Earth's surface.

If a bullet were fired from the gun at very low velocity, the bullet would fall to Earth following a sharp curve. Should the bullet be fired at higher velocity, it would still fall to Earth, but it would travel along a broader curve. At even greater velocity, the bullet would fall to Earth, but now its curve would be extremely broad, enough so the curve would match the curve of Earth's surface. The bullet would fall "around Earth"—it would be in orbit. Isaac Newton was right. In one second, the Moon moves forward 1020 meters, and it falls one millimeter toward Earth. In the same distance on Earth, the planet's surface curves one millimeter from a straight tangent. The two match very closely, so the Moon stays in orbit.

Following the same line of reasoning, the mystery of the orbiting planets can also be explained. For example, in one second, Earth falls about three millimeters toward the Sun.

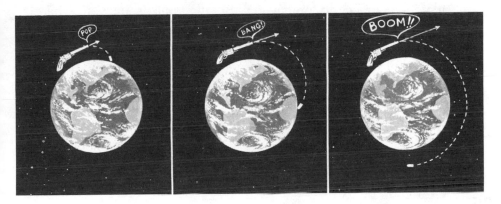

Isaac Newton proposed that bullets fired from a gun would move as shown.

Earth's forward velocity is 29.6 kilometers a second. The two motions cause Earth to remain in orbit around the Sun.

The same explanation applies to artificial Earth satellites. A satellite is carried to the elevation for which it is designed. Once there, rockets accelerate the satellite along a path tangent to Earth's surface. The velocity required is determined by altitude; satellites closer to Earth must move much faster than those farther out.

As the Moon and artificial satellites go around Earth and Earth goes around the Sun, our planet moves in other ways.

What is precession?

One of Earth's movements is called precession, which comes from *precede,* meaning to go before. If you have ever spun a gyroscope, you have observed precession. It is the swinging about of the axis of the gyroscope as it is pulled by Earth's gravity.

In a similar way, the axis of Earth is made to swing about as it is pulled by the Moon's gravity. If the pull were even, there would be no precession. But the pull is uneven. The greatest pull is on Earth's bulge, which is located along the equator. Earth is not truly spherical; the diameter of the equatorial bulge region is 22 kilometers greater than the polar diameter.

The axis of Earth is tilted to the Moon's path. The pull of the Moon on Earth's bulge attempts to put Earth's axis at right

The Moon pulls on Earth's bulge. As Earth resists the force, it precesses.

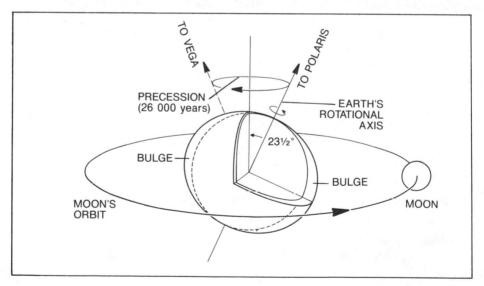

angles to the Moon's path. Since Earth is spinning, it resists the tendency and moves at a right angle to the Moon's pull; it precesses. Earth's axis therefore scribes out a circle in the sky, taking 26 000 years to complete one turn.

This means that the North Pole points to changing locations in the sky. Presently it is pointing in the direction of Polaris, the North Star. When the Egyptians were building the pyramids, the axis pointed more closely toward Thuban, a star in Draco. Some 12 000 years from now, the star nearest the pole will be Vega, in the constellation Lyra.

In addition, the poles of Earth shift in a small circle of 18 to 20 meters. This movement is another puzzle. Probably it is caused by shifts of large air masses, the flow of water in the oceans, or perhaps the movements of plates—the large sections of Earth's crust that move atop the magma beneath the surface.

Should this make you dizzy, there is good reason, for you and Earth move in many different ways. Earth rotates at 1600 kilometers an hour along the equator; it goes around the Sun 105 000 kilometers an hour; it drifts with the Sun toward the constellation Hercules 70 000 kilometers an hour. At the same time, it accompanies the Sun around the center of the galaxy some 250 000 kilometers an hour. And there is more. While our galaxy is rotating, it is also moving through space, perhaps going around other galaxies. Which galaxies they might be, and how fast all are moving, remain mysteries to be explored.

8 MOVEMENTS OF CONTINENTS AND SEAS

Right now you are moving in all the various ways mentioned in the last chapter. Also, if you live in North America, you are moving westward and northward. The whole continent is sliding along. So are all the continents and seas of the world, as well as the entire crust of the planet. The crust is made of separate sections, called plates, many of which are larger than entire continents. All the plates are moving, causing some to separate while others move closer together and even dig under one another. These motions, separations, and joinings set up the conditions that cause most earthquakes and volcanoes.

For centuries their occurrence had been perplexing. People had believed they were calamities caused by angry gods, to punish people for failing to make proper sacrifices or some other wrongdoing.

The edges of plates are weakened sections of Earth's crust. They are the locations where most volcanoes and earthquakes occur. DR. PAUL D. LOWMAN / NASA

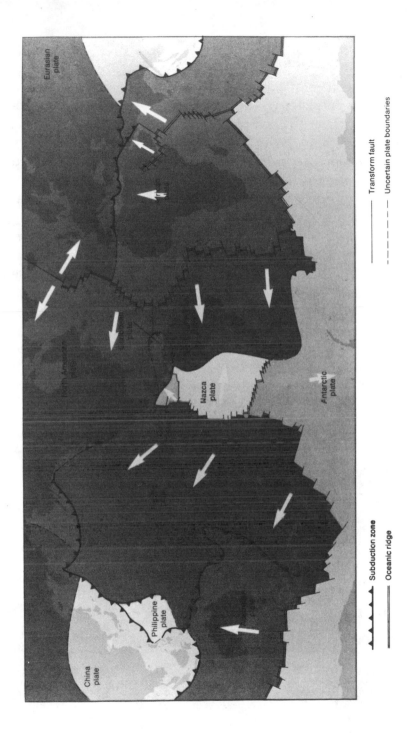

Subduction zone

Oceanic ridge

Transform fault

Uncertain plate boundaries

Eurasian plate

North American plate

Nazca plate

Antarctic plate

China plate

Philippine plate

What is tectonics?

A more correct solution came early in this century, with a theory called tectonics—the study of the structure and movements of large sections of Earth. The word means building and comes from *Tecton,* a carpenter in *The Iliad,* an ancient Greek poem. According to the theory, continents formed rather· recently in Earth's history. For several billion years, there were no continents. Or, if there were any, the formations came and went; they were not permanent. About 200 million years ago, the solid material combined and was surrounded by a single sea called Panthalassa, from *pan* meaning all, and *thalassa* meaning seas. Less than a quarter of the crust was above water. It was in the form of a single continent called Pangaea, meaning all the land. This was several million years before dinosaurs appeared.

Beneath Earth's crust, there is a semi-liquid layer called magma. The solid crust "floats" atop the magma. For reasons that still remain unexplained, the plates of the crust move about, some east or west, others north or south.

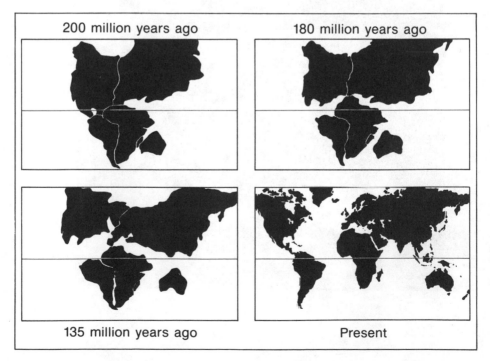

200 million years ago   180 million years ago

135 million years ago   Present

Pangaea held together for millions of years. Then, about 135 million years ago, stresses and strains, probably caused by uneven distribution of Earth's mass, caused Pangaea to split apart. Where there had been a single land mass, there were now two. The northern section was Laurasia; and the southern one, Gondwanaland, or simply Gondwana. This was during the Jurassic period, when dinosaurs flourished.

The motions continued so that, after roughly 70 million years, Laurasia and Gondwana had broken into pieces that had shapes somewhat like those of the continents known today.

The protocontinents, newly formed, continued to move in the directions shown in the drawing on page 46. North America moved away from Eurasia; South America and Africa separated. India moved northward to join Asia; Australia broke free from Antarctica and moved northeastward. During the Cenozoic period, the one in which we are now living and which began some 65 million years ago, the continents essentially took the shapes and positions they have today. However, these conditions are only temporary. Each year North America moves a centimeter or so away from Europe; Africa moves north toward Europe; and Australia continues to move northeastward. Eventually, the Earth map will look quite different than its present appearance.

Is there proof of plate movements?

In order for the tectonics theory to stand up, there must be observations, experiments, measurements, or something equally reliable to support it. There are a good many reasons for believing this theory is correct.

Lystrosaurus

In 1967, while scientists were making excavations at Coalsack Bluff in Antarctica, they made an exciting discovery. They found fossil remains of lystrosaurus: a chunky, sturdy, short-legged, stub-tailed, and blunt-nosed animal about the size of a dog. The creature was not unknown, for fossils of it had been found earlier in India and Africa. But finding fossils in Antarctica gave strong support to the theory that Africa, India, and Antarctica had been a single land body at the time lystrosaurus flourished. The animal could not have traveled across seas to get from one region to another because it was not a swimmer. The only way it could have gotten to Antarctica was overland. So the land masses had to have been unbroken or, if they were separate, a land bridge must have connected them.

Magnetism

Earth has a magnetic field. Lines of magnetic force run from pole to pole. When a piece of iron aligns with those force lines, the metal becomes magnetized. For example, hot water or steam radiators that have been in a generally north-south line for a few years are magnetized. This can be checked with a sensitive compass. If the north pole of the compass is brought near the northerly end of the radiator, the needle should be repulsed, because like poles repel.

Just as iron crystals form into north-south lines and become magnetized, so it is with certain metallic rock crystals. They line up in patterns geologists can "read" much as archaeologists "read" the fossils of plants and animals.

From their studies of rock crystals, geologists believe that Earth's magnetic field has switched back and forth many times.

Research ships have towed sensitive instruments along the ocean floor gathering information about magnetic variations. From these data they have been able to chart ancient magnetic fields. Invariably the pattern that develops on one side of a break or rift in Earth's crust is repeated almost exactly on the other side. This means that the rocks must have been joined when the patterns were developing. For example, the crystal patterns in rocks along the east coast of North America match very closely the patterns seen in rocks of the British Isles and western Europe.

In a similar vein, fossils of ancient sea life found along the shores of North America match, in many cases, those found along the European coast.

The mid-Atlantic ridge

Toward the center of the Atlantic Ocean, a mountain range extends some 18 000 kilometers north and south. Its curves and bends match very closely the curves of the continents that border the ocean.

Ocean research vessels have drilled into the range and into other regions of the ocean floor. They cut cores of rocks, which were then analyzed and dated.

The rocks found along the range, or the mid-Atlantic ridge as it is called, are younger than the rocks found closer to the continents. This discovery supports the plate theory of Earth's crust.

When the African and South American plates separated, the rift between them became a weakened part of the crust. Hot molten rock underneath the crust was able to push through the weakened section. Over millions of years, the lava pushed up the crust, making a ridge of mountains. The lava was "new" rock.

Sections of the ridge are still very active—new rock is still flowing up through it. Iceland, which is a part of the ridge, has had more than a dozen violent volcanic eruptions during the present century. In 1963, a whole new island was formed. Usually the eruptions along the ridge are completely underwater. But this one was so extensive that the lava and ash piled high enough to break through the surface of the sea. In a few weeks, the rock and ash had become an island 150 meters high and almost a kilometer across. Rumbling continued for several months. By the time the volcano had subsided, the island had grown to about two square kilometers. It has been called Surtsey, after Surtur, a mythological Icelandic creature who, according to legend, brought fire to the land.

Volcanoes and earthquakes

The mid-Atlantic ridge is raised and split, making a rift that formed as the North American and Eurasian plates separated. There are several plates in Earth's crust, and where they separated from one another, there are other rifts. The map on page 45 shows the locations of volcanoes and earthquakes that have occurred over the last few decades. They are strung along the mid-Atlantic rift and along other separations between plates. Or they are at locations where one plate is digging under another, disrupting surface structure and often weakening it so that magma pushes upward. That is what happened in 1980 to cause the Mount Saint Helens' eruption. Plates sliding past one another also produce earthquakes such

Eruptions of volcanoes, such as Mount Saint Helens, generally occur at the edge of plates. U.S. GEOLOGICAL SURVEY

as those experienced in California and along the west coast of South America.

When volcanoes or earthquakes are reported, notice where they are located. Very likely they will be somewhere along one of these plate separations. Most frequently they occur somewhere along the edge of the Pacific Ocean. An irregular line traced out along South America, western North America, the Aleutian Islands, Japan, and Indonesia marks the boundaries of what is called the ring of fire, the most active region of the planet.

There appears to be ample support of the tectonics theory. Earth is a dynamic world hurtling through space, moving in a complex number of ways while at the same time sections of the planet itself are moving.

9 MOTIONS OF THE AIR AND SEA

Why did people think Earth could not spin?

In the sixteenth century, Nicolaus Copernicus (1473–1543), a famous Polish scientist, attempted to solve mysteries for which many explanations had been offered down through the centuries—the location of Earth in space and how Earth moved. At that time, people believed Earth stood still; it did not spin, nor did it go around the Sun. Indeed, the Sun went around Earth, they said, as well as all the planets. Copernicus said the opposite was true. He said the Sun was at the center and all objects went around the Sun. As the objects revolved around the Sun, all of them were also spinning.

It was a startling idea, and one that many could not accept. If Earth was spinning, they argued, why didn't the wind blow all the time? Earth would slip by the air from west to east, so the wind should blow constantly in the other direction. Birds should be buffeted about and carried along in that direction. Clouds should always move eastward. It all seemed logical to them, but only because little was known about the movements of air and what caused them. They were riddles. Eventually they were solved, and so several arguments against the ideas of Copernicus disappeared.

The air blanket that surrounds Earth behaves in many ways as though it were fastened to the planet. As Earth rotates, so does the air. At the same time, there are multitudes of motions within the air blanket. For the most part, the motions are caused by the unequal heating of Earth's surface. For example, land surfaces heat up more quickly than does the surface of the sea. Therefore, air over the land gets warmer during the day than does air over the sea.

As the air becomes warmer, its density decreases. Colder air, which is more dense, digs under the warmer air, pushing it upward—the warmer air rises. Colder air blows in toward the warmer region; a breeze blows from the sea to the land.

What causes local weather?

Local breezes contribute to our weather. In addition, there are larger air movements, generally from west to east. Cooler air sweeps into the western United States from Canada, and warmer air comes in from the Gulf of Mexico and the South Pacific. The air masses sweep across the country, creating storms and disturbances wherever they meet. Tremendous amounts of energy are involved, for the air blanket weighs 4.5×10^{15} metric tons—4500 with 12 zeros after it.

There are many explanations for local weather: differences in ground cover, the presence of mountains or large cities, or nearness of large bodies of water. There are also worldwide movements caused by the uneven heating of the planet. Equatorial waters, for example, are a lot warmer than polar seas. And so the air along the equator is much warmer than polar air. All around the Earth, warm equatorial air rises and cooler air blows in toward the equator. These are called the prevailing winds, because they blow most of the time. They are also called the trade winds, because sailing ships traveling from Europe to America used those winds to blow them along. They were called the northeast trades, because they blew from the northeast to the southwest. Winds are named by the direction from which they blow.

What are the main motions of the air?

As hot tropical air rises, it cools. It also moves to higher latitudes, where the cooled denser air is pulled to Earth's surface. Once there, the air splashes north and south. The southward-moving portion becomes the trade winds. The air that moves northward becomes the westerlies—blowing from west to east.

The region where the air moves downward has been called the horse latitudes. It is generally located about 30 degrees north and south of the equator and is a region of calms. Sailing ships often became stranded in the region; they were becalmed. The name horse latitudes may have arisen in legends. According to one, ships that were carrying horses dumped them overboard to lessen the ship's weight and so made it possible to move more easily. Other stories say that horses were put overboard and hitched to the ship. They pulled the ship out of the calm region as they swam.

The map on page 55 shows the main movements of the atmosphere. If you place yourself at the tail of any of the arrows, facing the head, the wind veers to the right in the northern hemisphere and to the left in the southern half of the world. This is called the coriolis effect, after the Frenchman Gaspard G. de Coriolis, who, in 1835, explained how the rotation of Earth affects the motions of air, water, and any free-moving objects over the surface.

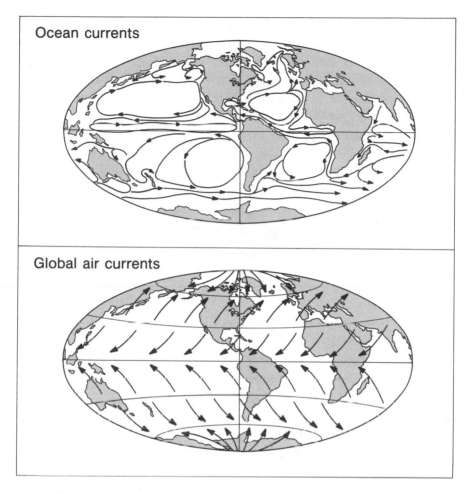

Differences in the temperature of masses of air cause them to move in the manner shown. The same is true for currents in the sea.

How do ocean currents move?

The map of Earth's oceans on page 55 shows major motions of the seas. Once again, the movement is toward the right north of the equator and to the left south of it. When this was found out, a long-standing mystery was solved—why Great

Britain is so warm even though it is quite far north of the equator. It is because of the Gulf Stream, a river of warm water that flows northward along the east coast of the United States, and continues around the edge of the North Atlantic Ocean.

The Gulf Stream is a river of water that is warmed in the equatorial zone. Heat in that water warms the air that blows over the British Isles. The warm air also picks up water vapor, which is then dropped as it goes overland. Rainfall in Scotland is high, 1420 millimeters on the average; it tapers off to 905 millimeters in England. In the northeastern United States, average rainfall varies from place to place; it is generally around 1000 millimeters.

What is climate?

Climate is average weather; it is the weather experienced in a region over a long period of time. The major aspect of climate is seasonal change, especially those changes that occur in the temperate zones. Long ago the changes could not be explained, although many suspected that somehow the Sun was responsible for them. Indeed it is so, for the main causes of all weather and climate are variations in solar radiation.

The Sun gives off essentially the same amount of energy year in and year out, as well as all through the year. Therefore, the changes must be caused by conditions here on Earth that affect the amount of radiation received. And they are. The primary factor is the tilt of Earth's axis. If our axis were at a right angle to a line connecting Earth and the Sun, weather throughout a year would remain just about unchanged, because radiation received by all regions of the planet would not vary.

How does Earth's tilt affect climate?

Earth's axis is tilted 23½ degrees from a line vertical to the Earth-Sun line. Throughout the year, Earth's axis remains tilted. At the present time, the axis points very close to Polaris, the North Star. During winter, the northern half of Earth is tilted away from the Sun. Much of the Sun's radiation glances off; it is not absorbed. Six months later, the northern half is tilted toward the Sun. At that angle, much more of the energy is absorbed, so the northern hemisphere becomes heated.

Spring and fall are transition seasons. The Earth is not tilted toward the Sun nor away from it. Earth is moving from winter to summer, in the northern hemisphere, or from summer to winter, in the southern hemisphere.

Mysteries of currents, weather, and climate have been pretty well solved, although we are a long way from knowing how to forecast weather with complete accuracy. The causes of weather and climate are understood. However, scientists continue to study movements of the oceans, air, and seas, hoping to better understand how they affect planet Earth.

What is acid rain?

There is a lot of acid in vinegar and lemon juice—they are sour. There is also acid in rain. Not very much, but a slight amount. And generally that is good, because most plants thrive on slightly acidic conditions. But when the amount becomes too great, plants perish. And so do fish, frogs, and other animals that live in lakes and ponds that are too acid.

Right now fish are dying in thousands of lakes in the northeastern United States, in Canada, and in other countries. The water is too acid. The acidity is caused by waste gases from factories and electric generating plants, mainly in the Ohio River valley. The factories burn fuel that gives off sulfur and

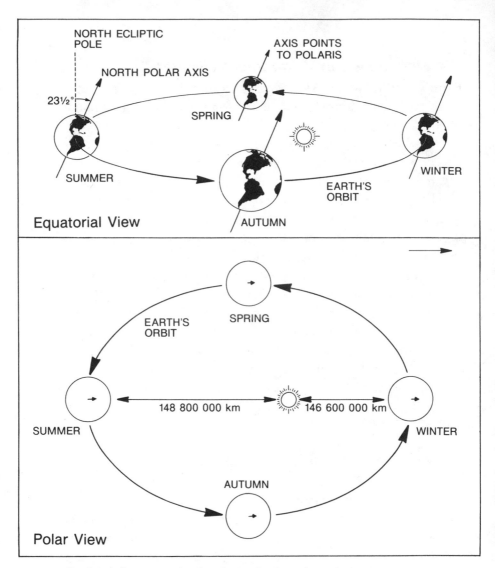

During July we are farther from the Sun than during January. In July the northern hemisphere absorbs more energy than it does in January.

nitrous oxides. Long ago, people in the area complained about the gases, so the chimneys were made higher. Now the gases go into the upper atmosphere, where winds generally blow from west to east. The waste products are carried hundreds of miles toward the northeast.

When sulfurous gases combine with water in the atmosphere, sulfuric acid is produced. It becomes part of the clouds. When rain falls from the clouds, so does the sulfuric acid. This is acid rain.

The same thing happens with nitrous gases. In this case, nitric acid is formed.

The condition is so bad that, in some places, lakes have no life in them. There may be a few large fish, but once they are gone, there will be no young to take their place. Also, trees around the lakes are dying.

Acid rain is caused by air pollution. If the condition is not corrected, results could be disastrous. The only way to solve the problem is to reduce pollution.

Some factories have put scrubbers into chimneys. These remove a lot of the sulfur, but they are not effective against nitrous gases, which still escape. It is much better to stop putting products into the air than to try to get them out. But that is not always easy.

Factories would have to burn coal and oil containing smaller amounts of sulfur and nitrous compounds. That means better and more expensive fuels must be used. Costs may go so high that factories cannot operate. Or they must find other sources of energy, such as nuclear power. But a good many people argue against that solution; they believe nuclear power causes more problems than it solves.

Scientists may find ways to clean waste gases by removing ash and dust particles and acid-making gases. Right now that is the only way to correct the situation. Meanwhile, acid rain continues to fall. Every day more fish die. More lakes and ponds become dead. They become filled with crystal clear acid-water in which no plants or animals can survive. Acid rain is no mystery, but it is a severe problem that must be resolved.

10 END OF EARTH

How does the Sun affect Earth?

Of all the planets, Earth is the most important to you and me. However, in the solar system it is insignificant. Earth is a lesser planet—Jupiter, Saturn, Uranus, and Neptune are much more massive. And more than 99 percent of the mass of the solar system is contained in the Sun; it overpowers the planets. Therefore, whatever happens to the Sun has notable effects on the planets. Just as the past history of Earth is connected with the Sun, Earth's future will be determined by what happens to this nearby star.

The Sun is a middle-aged star. It is probably some 5 billion years old, and it will continue to exist for at least another 5 billion years. During that time, many changes will occur, and they will have major effects on Earth.

What is the Sun's life history?

No one has ever been able to follow the entire life history of a star. They couldn't have. Stars last for billions of years, and modern man has been on the planet for only about a million years. However, astronomers look at thousands of stars, some older than the Sun and some younger, so they are able to see stages that they believe the Sun has passed through and will go through in the future. Also, astronomers work out theories that indicate how a star with the mass, composition, and temperature of the Sun will behave. So, using such theories, as well as their observations of other stars, astronomers have put together a life history of the Sun. And, in a sense, it is the story of planet Earth, its past and its future.

Presently the Sun is called a hydrogen-burning star. There is no actual burning of hydrogen in the sense of a chemical reaction producing fire. Rather, hydrogen is presently fueling nuclear-fusion reactions that create helium and that release a tremendous amount of energy—two billion times more than the total amount Earth receives from the Sun.

Billions of years ago, the materials that make up the Sun, mostly hydrogen and helium, were a huge gaseous cloud. Small clusters of molecules formed within that cloud, and gravitation of the clusters attracted and held other molecules. Increasing mass of the clusters meant increasing gravitation, and this meant even more molecules were attracted. The mass grew and grew to its present value—more than three hundred thousand times the mass of Earth. This was great enough to cause gravitational heating in the interior to reach 14 million degrees. The heat caused hydrogen nuclei to fuse together to become the nuclei of helium atoms, releasing energy in the process. The gaseous mass had become a star.

During its early stages, the Sun's radiation was uneven. But for the past several millenniums, the Sun has been shining steadily except for a few short-lived minor variations. And so Earth has been receiving a more or less steady and even supply of energy, enough to hold its temperature at 14°C year after year. Steady conditions during the past few billion years have enabled life to appear on the planet and to evolve into the multitude of plants and animals that exists today.

What is Earth's destiny?

It seems that such a vast ecological system as that which exists on Earth among the plants, animals, air, water, and land would go on forever. But it won't. Eventually, drastic changes will occur.

Each second, 564 million tons of the Sun's hydrogen go out of existence. Five hundred sixty million tons become helium, and 4 million tons are converted into energy. It would seem that the disappearance of so much hydrogen would cause the Sun to burn out quickly. But it is so massive that the process will continue for perhaps another 3 billion years. By then, so much hydrogen will be used up, the hydrogen-helium reaction will slow down. Forces pushing matter outward will weaken, and gravitational force will become dominant. This will cause the star to collapse. As it collapses, density will increase rapidly and so will temperature.

This brief stage of collapse will be followed by expansion. Soaring temperature will cause the outer part of the star to become much larger than it was previously. Energy given off by the expanded star will come from a greatly enlarged surface, however, and so the star will appear redder and cooler. The Sun will have become a red giant. That will be quite a change from its present category, which is that of a yellow dwarf.

When the Sun becomes a giant, its diameter may increase a hundred times over its present 1.5 million kilometers. It may extend beyond Earth's orbit; our planet would be inside the Sun.

As the expanding Sun approaches Earth, rocks and soil will become very hot. All life will have long since perished. Much of the atmosphere will be blown away. Still, there will be enough for rain to form, although it will be boiling hot. Rapid evaporation from the steaming oceans will add water to the air and there will be steady, torrential rains—steaming and boiling.

As Earth is surrounded by the Sun, temperatures will go up and up. Eventually the atmosphere will be lost, water will change to vapor and so will the solid portions of the planet. The stuff of Earth will change to gases and be swallowed by the Sun. The planet will cease to exist. Only the outer planets will survive.

But there is no need to worry. These dire events are scheduled for the long-term future, billions of years from now.

After the Sun has engulfed Earth, the star will continue to change. It will collapse once more, this time probably reaching only a fraction of its present size, no larger than Earth is now. Fusion will have long ceased. Heat will now come from gravitational collapse. But even that source will end. The Sun will cool and become a solitary, cold, black-dwarf star.

Meanwhile other stars will have formed. Some will be hydrogen-burning, just as the Sun once was. It is likely that among these new stars there will be at least one with planets not unlike Earth. And who knows, life may appear on one of those planets much as it did on Earth. The cycle goes on, down through eternity.

FURTHER READING

Branley, Franklyn M. *Mysteries of the Planets.* New York: Lodestar Books, 1988.

Fisher, David E. *The Birth of the Earth: A Wanderlied Through Space, Time, and the Human Imagination.* New York: Columbia University Press, 1987.

Lambert, David. *Planet Earth.* New York: Franklin Watts, 1983.

Sheffield, Charles. *Earthwatch: A Survey of the World from Space.* New York: Macmillan, 1981.

Whipple, Fred L. *Orbiting the Sun: Planets and Satellites of the Solar System.* Cambridge: Harvard University Press, 1981.

INDEX

Page numbers in *italics* refer to illustrations.